HEY GOD, I'M IN THIS DEN SO YOU LET ME EAT THIS GUY NAMED DANIEL?!

THE LION TELLS HIS SIDE OF THE STORY

TROY SCHMIDT

ILLUSTRATED BY CORY JONES

LOOK, I'M A LION. THE KING OF THE BEASTS.
AND WHAT DO LIONS LIKE TO DO? EAT!
AND WHEN A LION CAN'T EAT, HE GETS CRANKY.
GRRRGGGGGGRRRLLLLGRRGGGLLLL.
HEAR THAT SOUND? OH, IT'S A GROWL ALL RIGHT,
BUT IT'S NOT FROM MY MOUTH—IT'S FROM MY STOMACH!
THAT'S WHAT HAPPENED WHEN I GOT THROWN INTO THIS DEN
AND GOD TOLD ME I COULDN'T EAT THIS GUY NAMED DANIEL.
LET ME TELL YOU MY SIDE OF THE STORY.

GRRRR

NOW WE KING OF THE BEASTS KNOW THAT THERE'S A GOD,
BUT SOMETIMES WE FORGET TO PRAY TO HIM
BECAUSE, WELL, WE'RE KINGS.
BUT AT THIS POINT, I DIDN'T FEEL MUCH LIKE A KING.
SO I DID WHAT DANIEL DID. I PRAYED.
"HEY GOD, I'M STARVING IN THIS DEN, SO WHY WON'T
YOU LET ME EAT THIS GUY NAMED DANIEL?!"
"BECAUSE HE'S A VERY IMPORTANT MAN
WHO DOESN'T FORGET TO PRAY TO ME, EVEN THOUGH
HE'S VERY IMPORTANT," GOD REPLIED.

"YOU SEE," GOD TOLD ME, "EVEN THOUGH HE'S ONE OF THE HIGHEST RANKING PEOPLE IN HIS KINGDOM, HE REMEMBERED ME AND PRAYED TO ME. HE DIDN'T WORRY ABOUT HIS NEEDS, BUT MINE. AND I WASN'T ABOUT TO LET YOU EAT HIM, SO I HAD AN ANGEL SHUT YOUR MOUTHS."

WOW. I REALIZED THEN THAT I WAS NOTHING LIKE DANIEL. I FELT LIKE A KING, BUT I TOOK WHAT I WANTED. I HAD NEVER MET ANYONE AS POWERFUL AS DANIEL WHO TURNED TO GOD.

I THINK PEOPLE CALL IT *HUMILITY*. I'VE HEARD THAT WORD BEFORE BUT NEVER HAD MUCH USE FOR IT. IT DESCRIBED DANIEL, THOUGH, HOW HE RESPECTED GOD FIRST, NO MATTER HOW IMPORTANT HE WAS. AND GOD TOOK CARE OF HIM.